The Library of
ASTRONAUT BIOGRAPHIES™

NEIL ARMSTRONG

The First Man on the Moon

Ann Byers

rosen
central™

The Rosen Publishing Group, Inc., New York

jB
ARMSTRONG

Published in 2004 by The Rosen Publishing Group, Inc.
29 East 21st Street, New York, NY 10010

Library of Congress Cataloging-in-Publication Data

Byers, Ann.
Neil Armstrong: the first man on the moon / Ann Byers. – 1st ed.
    p. cm —(The library of astronaut biographies)
Summary: Discusses the life and training as an astronaut of Neil Armstrong, the first man to set foot on the moon.
Includes bibliographical references and index.
ISBN 0-8239-4461-1 (library binding)
1. Armstrong, Neil, 1930– —Juvenile literature. 2. Astronauts—United States—Biography—Juvenile literature. [1. Armstrong, Neil, 1930– 2. Astronauts.] I. Title. II. Series.
TL789.85.A75B96 2004
629.45'0092—dc22

                                                    2003014301

Manufactured in the United States of America

CONTENTS

LOOKING SKYWARD

The Roaring Twenties—a postwar decade of wild parties, jazz, illegal alcohol, and prosperity in the United States—came to a sudden, screeching halt with the stock market crash of 1929. The Great Depression would put its stamp on the 1930s in the way that flappers and gangsters had characterized the 1920s. The first full year of the Depression—1930—was a very hard one worldwide. In the United States alone, millions of people were out of work. Banks failed, factories closed, and personal savings evaporated.

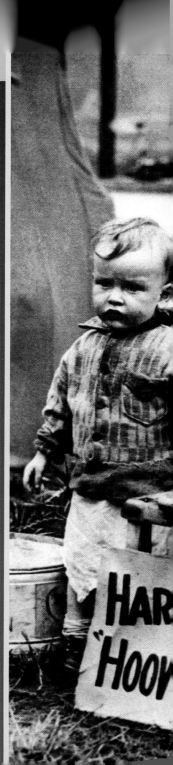

HAR "Hoov

HOOVER'S
POOR FARM
TOBACCO
FUND

...MES ARE STILL
...NG OVER US

This photo was taken in July 1932 when one-fourth of the workforce in America was unemployed. These signs illustrate people's displeasure with President Herbert Hoover's policies during the early years of the Great Depression.

Even in the greatest of difficulties, however, Americans have always continued to dream. They have always envisioned a brighter future and worked hard to make it a reality. In 1930, while standing in long bread lines and huddling outside soup kitchens, impoverished Americans looked to the skies and dreamed big.

Only three years earlier, the pioneering pilot Charles Lindbergh had shown that airplanes could carry people through the sky, across the Atlantic Ocean to Europe and back. Americans now dreamed of someday getting the chance to fly in those planes. People who had recently seen the automobile revolutionize their everyday lives and change the way the country did business began to imagine how airplane travel might also transform society. The car had given rise to a number of related industries—steel, rubber, and petroleum. It had also opened up the country for travel by ordinary citizens. Previously, people were far less mobile. Relatively few people journeyed more than 100 miles (161 kilometers) beyond their community until the car set them free to roam the country. Perhaps air travel would also unlock a new frontier of technology and adventure.

Even as the Depression took hold and the news seemed to go from bad to worse, Americans were treated to an awe-inspiring distraction that seemed to point to a better tomorrow. In 1930, Lindbergh again proved in dramatic fashion that air travel was both possible and practical. In that year, he set a world aviation speed record by flying from Los Angeles to

Above, spectators in London, England, watch pilot Charles Lindbergh land his plane, the *Spirit of St. Louis*, in May 1927. Several days earlier, Lindbergh had crossed the Atlantic Ocean in thirty-three hours and thirty minutes. This was the first nonstop flight across the Atlantic in history.

New York in fourteen hours and forty-five minutes. People dreamed of going faster still, and technology would soon grant that wish. In that same year of difficulty and dreams—1930—a British pilot obtained a patent for the very first turbojet engine.

In addition to flying faster, Americans dreamed of soaring higher. Military planes, the world's most advanced aircraft, flew at far higher altitudes than civilian airplanes, reaching heights of 17,000 feet (5,182 meters). In 1930, however, a new record was set—30,000 feet (9,144 m).

Could airplanes be made to fly even higher? Scientist Robert H. Goddard thought so. He believed that planes could travel as far as the Moon. He designed rockets that could propel planes farther and faster than gasoline engines could. In 1930, he launched an 11-foot (3.3-m) liquid-fueled rocket 2,000 feet (610 m) into the sky at a speed of 500 miles per hour (805 kilometers per hour). While he did not set a record for height, he did demonstrate the power and potential of rocket engines. It would not be long before the sky was no longer the limit. Soon, what was beyond the sky— outer space—would be humanity's new frontier.

Americans were already very interested in space by 1930. In that year, an American astronomer discovered the planet Pluto, 3 billion miles (4.8 billion km) from the Sun. Could rockets ever travel that far? A group of people who believed space travel was possible came together in April 1930 to form the American Interplanetary

This photo from 1932 shows Robert H. Goddard, a physics professor at Clark University in Worcester, Massachusetts, posing with a model rocket. Goddard worked on rocket experiments for seventeen years and was one of the first scientists to state the belief that rocket travel was possible.

Society, later renamed the American Rocket Society. Its purpose was to promote interest and experimentation in space travel and exploration.

In 1930, with jobs and fortunes being lost every day and with automobile production at half the level of the previous year, Americans could only dream of someday having the resources necessary to conquer the skies and the heavens beyond. In that same year, however, a child was born who would live those dreams. One day, Neil Armstrong would travel 140 times as fast as Lindbergh's 1930 record. He would fly 240,000 miles (386,243 km) higher than the highest plane reached in 1930. He would be lifted to that altitude by a rocket twenty-five times as big as Goddard's 11-foot (3.3-m) rocket. Merely a fantastic dream in 1930, a Moon landing became a reality almost forty years later when Neil Armstrong became the first person to fly to the Moon, walk on its surface, and return safely home to Earth. In the process, he would soar faster, higher, and farther than any human being before him.

CHAPTER 1

A DREAM TAKES HOLD

Airplanes were rare sights in the little town of Wapakoneta, Ohio, in the 1930s. Wapakoneta was a farming community, miles away from the nearest large city, so few planes ever flew overhead. On the edge of that quiet little town, on his grandparents' farm, Neil Armstrong was born on August 5, 1930.

Armstrong did not stay long in Wapakoneta. His father, Stephen, was a state auditor, and he had to travel to many of the state's counties to examine their financial records. Since it could take a year or more to audit each county's books, Stephen and

Neil's mother, Viola, with Neil and his younger brother and sister moved quite often.

Making the best of their unsettled home life, Stephen Armstrong was always looking for ways to expand his children's horizons and expose them to new things. In 1932, airplanes were still a pretty new and awe-inspiring sight. So when Neil was only two years old, his father took him to the National Air Races when the event came to Cleveland, Ohio. Four years later, the Armstrongs were living in Warren, Ohio, when Neil's father saw the opportunity to provide his six-year-old son with another new and exciting experience: an actual airplane ride. Neil sailed through the air in a Ford Trimotor, a small, three-engine plane that could barely fly more than 100 mph (161 km/h). Unlike most airplanes of that era, it was made of light metal instead of wood, so it was nicknamed the Tin Goose.

Because he was so young at the time, Neil Armstrong does not remember the air races or the ride in the Tin Goose, but many of his earliest memories are related to his fascination with aviation. He read aviation magazines such as *Flight, Air Trails,* and *Model*

Photographer Layne Kennedy took this picture of a Ford Trimotor airplane taking off from the EAA Air Adventure Museum. The Trimotor was a powerful, three-engine plane made of metal. In the 1930s, most planes had only one engine and were made of wood. The plane could hold twelve passengers, who sat in wicker chairs.

Airplanes. He packed several notebooks with his research on every kind of plane ever built up to that time. He wrote down the name of the aircraft, all the technical information he could find about it, and how it performed. Armstrong's room was filled with airplane models that he had built. He did not have much money, so he made the planes out of whatever he could get his hands on: paper, straw, scraps of

AN AEROSPACE
ENGINEER IS BORN

Neil Armstrong's high school physics class provided him with one of his first opportunities to test his airplane design skills. As part of a class project, he decided to build a wind tunnel. A wind tunnel is a tool airplane designers use to test the effect of air currents on a particular aircraft design. It is a passageway through which air is forced. A scale model airplane is suspended in the tunnel, allowing the designer to observe how the shape of the plane's body, the placement of the wings, and other design features respond to the gusts of air.

Neil's wind tunnel was a great success. More important, it allowed him to test some of his own airplane designs. He experimented with a device on the fan's motor that would allow air to flow through the tunnel at different speeds. While tinkering, he blew out a number of fuses in his home trying to perfect his project.

wood. His models were powered by rubber-band engines. Aviation had become an obsession for Neil. By the age of eight or nine, he knew that he wanted to do something with airplanes when he grew up.

Neil loved the idea of being in the sky. As a child, he often dreamed that he could make himself hover above the ground simply by holding his breath. He was far more than a dreamer, however. He truly believed that he could and would realize his dream of designing and piloting planes. So he set to work to make his dream come true.

Learning to Fly

Even though he loved building and designing airplane models, Neil wanted to do more than work with tiny, flightless replicas of the jets he studied so closely. He was itching to fly the real thing, and that desire was beginning to look more and more possible to satisfy. At a tiny airport just north of Wapakoneta, instructors were offering flying lessons.

The lessons cost $9 per hour, however—a steep sum in the mid-1940s. Neil's parents, with three children to care for, did not have the extra money

for flying lessons. So fifteen-year-old Neil went out and found a job, stocking shelves after school—first at a grocery store and later at a hardware store. After these jobs ended, he worked in a drugstore, stocking shelves and sweeping the floor before school and returning in the afternoon and on Saturdays to wait on customers. He often had to do his homework between serving customers. As soon as he had saved enough money, Neil enrolled in a flight class.

Whenever Neil had a day off, he hitchhiked the 3 miles (4.8 km) to the little airport. While his schoolmates were learning to drive cars, he was steering a yellow, two-seater Aeronca Champion high above their heads. On his sixteenth birthday, when his friends received their driver's licenses, Neil earned his student pilot's license.

A Golden Opportunity

In 1946, at about the same time Neil Armstrong was taking his first solo flight above the farms of Wapakoneta, the United States military was facing a problem that would become a golden opportunity for this small-town boy. World War II had ended a

Neil Armstrong *(circled)* began his career as a pilot very early, when he was still in his teens. Here he sits with a group of fellow pilots at the airport in Wapakoneta, Ohio, where he received his first flying lessons.

year earlier, and young men were no longer enlisting in the armed forces. The government was becoming increasingly worried that the armed forces would not have enough soldiers and sailors to defend the nation or its allies if another conflict suddenly broke out. The military wanted to increase its reserves by signing up men who would be trained and ready in case they were needed.

The navy, which operated its fleets of fighter jets on floating aircraft carriers around the world, soon developed a plan to build up its air reserves. Called the Hollaway program, it offered young men a chance to go to college for free in return for military service. It was a seven-year scholarship program. For the first two years, the navy would pay tuition, fees, and room and board at any college the young man chose. The student would be on "reserve" status—technically serving in the navy but called up to active duty only if a war or some other emergency required his service. After the first two years of college study, the young man would then be on active duty for the next three years. Following this period of active navy service, he would then return to reserve status and finish his final two years of college, paid for by the navy.

Many high school students tried to take advantage of the Hollaway program because it offered a free college education. Unlike many applicants, who felt it was the unpleasant price to pay for a free college education, Neil was drawn to the program's military service. Neil recognized that the program would give him a shot at flying military airplanes, the most advanced and exciting aircraft of all. When he was awarded the Hollaway scholarship, he chose to attend Purdue University in West Lafayette, Indiana, because it had an aeronautical engineering program. The "Holly Plan" would allow Neil to become an airplane designer and a pilot at the same time. It was truly a dream come true.

CHAPTER 2

IN THE AIR

According to the terms of the "Holly Plan," under ordinary circumstances Neil Armstrong should have been in college in the spring of 1949. A war in Korea was on the horizon, however, so Armstrong was called to active duty early. He was plucked from the classroom during his second year of college and immediately placed in naval flight school.

After learning how to fly using puddle jumpers—small, light planes—in Ohio, Armstrong was eager to get behind the controls of powerful military jets. That thrill would have to wait for four more months, however. First, Armstrong would have to attend ground school where navy pilots spent hours in the classroom studying the planes they would eventually fly. Before jeopardizing their lives and very expensive machinery in actual flight situations, the students needed to understand and master the cockpit's complex electronic equipment and instruments. They also had to learn how to navigate using the stars, instruments, and compass as guides.

After ground school came basic training, which Armstrong had been eagerly anticipating. In this period, he was finally given the opportunity to fly some of the world's very best planes. He flew alone and he flew in formation with other planes. He learned how to perform aerobatics (flying maneuvers such as rolls and dives), drop bombs, launch rockets, and fire a mounted machine gun.

When he had mastered all the mechanics involved in piloting naval aircraft, Armstrong was sent to advanced flight training. Here he performed all the same maneuvers and tasks, but this time he did them in jets based on an aircraft carrier. During advanced training, Armstrong proved himself to be a highly skilled pilot. He had no problem flying from either a landing strip or a carrier's deck. By the time he completed his advanced training, the Korean War had begun.

Fighter Pilot

The Korean War began in June 1950, when Communist North Korea invaded democratic South Korea. The United Nations voted to send troops in support of South Korea, with the majority of the military power supplied by the United States.

Just two years out of high school, Neil Armstrong was suddenly in sole command of one of the most deadly, powerful weapons the United States had— an F9F Panther. This fighter jet could travel 1,300 miles (2,092 km) at a top speed of almost 600 mph (966 km/h) without refueling. It held four cannons, each of which could fire 200 rounds of ammunition in a matter of seconds. In addition, the Panther could either drop two 1,000-pound (454-kilogram) bombs or shoot six rockets. This was a powerful machine and a huge responsibility for a twenty-year-old.

Above is an F9F Panther jet touching down on the deck of the USS *Oriskany* in 1952. Neil Armstrong flew this kind of plane from the aircraft carrier the USS *Essex* from 1950 to 1952 during the Korean War.

It was a responsibility that Armstrong shouldered with grace and ease. From his base on the aircraft carrier the USS *Essex*, his missions took him toward the eastern coast of North Korea and included the bombing of bridges, trains, and tanks. On several occasions, he shot down enemy fighters. In two years of service, Armstrong flew seventy-eight combat missions and was awarded the Air Medal and two Gold Stars. Medals were given for bravery in the face of danger. Many times Armstrong returned from missions with bullet holes in his plane. He simply patched up the holes, painted them over, and set off on the next mission. Once, his plane was damaged so badly that he barely made it back to the carrier.

It was a very close call, one of his first as an aviator, and it would not be the last. Yet Armstrong would remain as eager as ever to get back into the cockpit. His experiences in the air over Korea only increased his love of planes. They strengthened his determination to make aircraft design and operation his life's work.

When he was discharged from active duty in 1952, he returned to Purdue University to complete his studies in aeronautical engineering. He received his degree in 1955 and began looking for a job. His dream was still to create the sturdiest, fastest, and most powerful aircraft possible and fly that craft farther and higher than anyone had ever done before him.

CHAPTER 3

FLYING HIGH

When Neil Armstrong graduated from college with his aeronautical engineering degree, a number of companies wanted to hire this young, bright, and talented war veteran. The job he most wanted was at the High-Speed Flight Station of the National Advisory Committee for Aeronautics (NACA), at Edwards Air Force Base in California. This was a government agency that employed civilians as research scientists and test pilots. Though there was no opening at Edwards, NACA was interested in Armstrong and instead offered him a position at its Lewis Flight Propulsion Laboratory in Cleveland, Ohio, less than three hours from his hometown.

Of all the many job offers he received, the one at NACA paid the least. The agency was developing the most creative, exciting aircraft imaginable, though, and it was taking those planes beyond the limits anyone thought possible. This was a chance not only to design the aircraft of the future but also to fly them. Armstrong enthusiastically accepted the job.

At Lewis, the research scientists looked at problems airplanes continued to experience and tried to find solutions to them. One of those problems was the formation of ice on the planes' wings. In order to test deicing methods, Armstrong would first have to fly over Lake Erie in rain and snow so that ice would develop on his aircraft's wings. Then he would experiment with the various deicing systems NACA had created, learning which was the best for keeping the plane's wings clear. Sometimes he flew a Twin Mustang fighter jet over the Atlantic Ocean and launched rockets into the sea, testing the performance of both the rockets and the jets. The results of these tests would give him and his fellow engineers the information they would need to design and develop better rockets and planes.

While working for the National Advisory Committee for Aeronautics (NACA; NASA's predecessor), Neil Armstrong test piloted over 200 experimental jets, including some of the ones shown here at the NACA High Speed Flight Station. Clockwise from far left are the D-558-II, XF-92A, X-5, X-1, X-4, and the D-558-I.

Though thrilled with his work, Armstrong did not stay long in Cleveland. After just a few months, the job he wanted at the High-Speed Flight Station in California became available. He gladly packed up and drove across the country to Edwards Air Force Base, where he would now be working on the very latest in aircraft technology.

The High-Speed Flight Station housed every conceivable kind of aircraft. In his seven years there as a test pilot and design engineer, Armstrong would fly fighter planes, jets, helicopters, gliders, rocket planes, and X planes (experimental aircraft). He tested more than 200 different types of planes: the B-47 Stratojet bomber; the B-29 Superfortress, which launched rocket planes; the Thunderflash jet; the F-100 Super Sabre, the first plane he flew faster than the speed of sound; the F-101 Voodoo; and the X-1 rocket plane.

Another Close Call

One new flight-control system Armstrong helped develop for the X-15 featured a single control that could perform two jobs. Older models had used two joysticks—one for aerodynamic control and one for reaction control. The aerodynamic control allowed the pilot to maneuver the plane when it was in Earth's atmosphere, but it did not work at all in the near vacuum of space. The reaction control was for use above Earth's atmosphere. With the two-control system, pilots had to switch back and forth between

THE X-15

By far the most exotic plane at Edwards was the experimental X-15. It was a rocket plane that was hoisted to the sky under the wing of a B-52, then thrust free of the bomber, propelled forward and upward by a rocket. The rocket powered the plane for a minute or two until its fuel was spent. After the rocket had finished firing, the plane became a glider. Other than the rocket, it had no source of power, so it could only glide back down to Earth. In tests of the X-15, the pilot worked the controls of the aircraft and brought it to a dead-stick (without power) landing on the 25-mile-long (40-km-long) "runway" of Rogers Dry Lake in California's Mojave Desert. The average flight lasted ten minutes.

The X-15 broke all aviation records for altitude and speed. In one flight, Armstrong soared 207,500 feet (63,246 m) above Earth. In another, he zoomed at 4,000 mph (6,437 km/h), nearly six times the speed of sound (Mach 5.74; Mach 1 is the speed of sound). In order to test the plane's various systems and capabilities, he flew it in ways that simulated difficult or emergency conditions.

the two joysticks. The device Armstrong was testing combined aerodynamic and reaction controls in one stick.

The new device included a feature—the G limiter—that prevented the plane from accelerating beyond five Gs (five times the force of gravity felt on Earth). An acceleration that placed more than five times the normal force of gravity upon a pilot might lead to disorientation, dizziness, blackouts, and loss of

Test pilot Scott Crossfield *(left)* hands over the keys to the newly revamped rocket airplane X-15 to Major Robert White *(center)* and Neil Armstrong *(right)* in February 1961 at Edwards Air Force Base in California. The new model had a larger, more powerful engine. White would pilot the X-15 to a new air speed record of 2,275 miles (3,661 km) per hour.

control of the aircraft. Armstrong's assignment was to test this feature and make sure it worked properly. He had successfully tested the G limiter many times in a simulator, but this was to be the first real flight test. Once in the air, Armstrong had a hard time getting the X-15 up to five Gs. In the attempt, the plane sailed out of Earth's atmosphere. He still had some ability to guide the plane with the reaction controls, but he could not steer back down into the atmosphere because there was no air to "bite into." All he could do was let gravity do the work for him and wait until the plane dropped low enough on its own. Once gravity pushed it back into the density of Earth's atmosphere, the heavier airflow would allow him to gain control of the steering again.

When the X-15 finally reentered Earth's atmosphere, Armstrong discovered that he had drifted far off course and was miles away from the landing site at Rogers Dry Lake. Since the X-15 had no engine, it was no simple matter to correct his flight path and glide all the way back to the desert landing strip. Still, he somehow managed to turn the aircraft around and put it down safely at

Edwards. It was the longest X-15 flight on record . . . and the scariest for Neil Armstrong!

Personal Strength

This and similar hair-raising high-altitude incidents earned Armstrong a reputation for being exceptionally calm under pressure. He was also known as an extremely intelligent and talented engineer, especially after earning a master's degree in aerospace engineering from the University of Southern California. Most people thought of Armstrong as a very private person. He was quiet, shy, and somewhat of a loner. Instead of staying close to the base where he worked, he lived an hour away with his wife, Jan, in a small, simple cabin high in the San Gabriel Mountains. This man who flew ultramodern planes into the stratosphere chose, when on Earth, to live in a cabin without electricity or running water.

The cabin was a happy place, a retreat from the pressures of a high-stress job. While living there, Jan gave birth to two children, Ricky in 1957 and Karen in 1959. (A second son, Mark,

Neil Armstrong poses with his family on June 30, 1969. His older son, Ricky, stands behind his wife, Jan, and younger son, Mark, in their home in Houston, Texas.

was born in 1963.) But in 1961, the cabin became a place of sorrow. Karen was diagnosed with a brain tumor that could not be removed in an operation. All the doctors could do was try to shrink it. Armstrong took time off work to be with her during the treatments, which were not working. Shortly before Karen's third birthday, on Neil and Jan's sixth wedding anniversary, their only daughter died.

Private and solitary even in sorrow, Armstrong mourned for Karen in his own personal way. Then he returned to work.

Opportunities

On July 29, 1958, President Dwight D. Eisenhower signed into law the National Aeronautics and Space Act, signaling to the world that the United States was firmly committed to sending men into space. Succeeding NACA, the National Aeronautics and Space Administration (NASA) was established in October 1958 as a governmental agency committed to manned spaceflight and exploration. The agency hit the ground running with a $100 million budget, numerous facilities, and 8,000 employees. NACA's former emphasis on high–altitude flight shifted to NASA's quest to design manned spacecraft that would soar among the stars. While rockets and space-craft began to be designed and the space agency planned a series of manned spaceflight programs, the search began for NASA's first group of space pilots.

President Dwight D. Eisenhower *(second from left)* swears in Dr. T. Keith Glennan *(second from right)* as the first administrator of the newly formed NASA and Dr. Hugh L. Dryden *(far left)* as the space agency's deputy administrator. The ceremony took place at the White House on August 19, 1958.

Armstrong was not interested at first. He knew that flying in space would be much different from flying the X-15. The spaceships that had been launched up to that point—all unmanned—had been operated by people on the ground. He did not want to fly in any vehicle that he could not control himself. The pilot was the "eyes and ears" of a mission, and Armstrong felt that the pilot had to be able to react to conditions that ground controllers might not be able to see or understand from behind their computer monitors. If astronauts were going to be merely passengers, not pilots, he did not want to be an astronaut. Besides, the first call for astronauts went out to military test pilots, and Armstrong was now a civilian (someone not currently a member of the armed forces).

In 1961, only two years after the first NASA astronauts were selected, the space agency's Mercury project succeeded in launching Alan Shepard beyond Earth's atmosphere into zero gravity, making him the first American in space. In that same year, John Glenn became the first American to orbit Earth, circling it three times in a Mercury spacecraft over which he had limited piloting control.

USS LAKE CHAMPLAIN

Astronaut Alan B. Shepard inspects his space capsule following his return from America's first ever manned spaceflight in 1961. Following splashdown in the Atlantic Ocean, Shepard and his Mercury capsule were recovered and brought to the USS *Champlain*, which was stationed nearby.

Glenn's pioneering spaceflight changed Armstrong's thinking. He realized that astronauts were not simply riding in spacecraft for publicity purposes. They were actually piloting these capsules and helping to design them. When a second call for astronauts was made by NASA in 1962, Armstrong knew what he had to do. He and another test pilot discussed the various opportunities open to them. "You can do what you want," Armstrong told his friend, "but space is the frontier, and that is where I intend to go" (as quoted in Andrew Choikin's *A Man on the Moon*). In the spring of that year, Neil Armstrong applied to NASA's astronaut training program. His childhood dream of floating free, far beyond Earth, was about to come true.

CHAPTER 4

AIMING HIGHER

By the time Neil Armstrong applied to the astronaut corps in 1962, the space race was already five years old. The space race was an unofficial contest between the United States and the Soviet Union (modern-day Russia and other former Soviet republics) to be the first to explore and make use of space. The two superpowers were deep in the midst of the Cold War—a decades-long period of simmering distrust and tension.

The United States and the Soviet Union were enemies that were sharply divided philosophically. The United States believed in democracy and capitalism, in which people are free to choose their

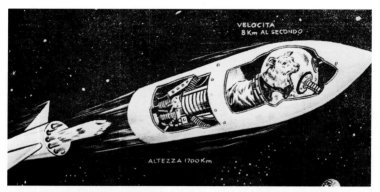

At top is a cartoon from an Italian newspaper showing *Sputnik II* and its dog occupant. *Sputnik II* was the second major Soviet triumph in space and highlighted the shortcomings of the American space program. At bottom, men in Toronto, Canada, read about the failed U.S. Vanguard missile in 1957. The headlines read "Ike's Sputnik is Dudnik" and "U.S. Moon Dud." "Ike" was a nickname for U.S. president Dwight D. Eisenhower.

own government and engage in the buying and selling of goods with minimal government interference. The Soviet Union believed in Communism, which saw government's role as making all its people equal, in part by controlling the flow of money and commerce so that extremes of wealth and poverty would no longer exist. Both nations wished to export their philosophies to other countries and create a world of like-minded nations. In order to block each other's international efforts, both nations began collecting large stockpiles of weapons, including nuclear bombs and missiles. A tense military standoff developed between the two superpowers and their allies.

This arms race soon spread into space. If either country could successfully launch a craft into space, it could become a platform for spy cameras or weapons. The space race became an important military venture and a matter of national security. That is why the first astronauts were drawn from the armed services.

When Armstrong entered the space program in 1962, the United States was losing the space race. The Soviet Union had thrust the first satellite—

Sputnik I—into orbit three months before NASA could launch one of its own. The Soviets had put a man in space three weeks before the United States did, and that man had circled Earth nearly a year before John Glenn performed the same feat. U.S. politicians and military leaders were embarrassed to have fallen behind the Soviets and were genuinely afraid that the Soviet Union might come to dominate the new frontier. If it were able to achieve that, it might then be able to control events on Earth from the high ground of space.

In this tense atmosphere, John F. Kennedy, the newly elected president of the United States, called on Congress in May 1961 to increase spending for the space program. He said, "I believe this nation should commit itself, before this decade is out, to landing a man on the Moon and returning him safely to the Earth." Congress agreed and gave NASA additional money, with the understanding that the space agency would figure out a way to reach the Moon in less than nine years.

NASA's first seven astronauts had worked in the Mercury program, which was designed to prove that a human being could be sent into

The Mercury Seven astronauts inspect a model of the rocket that would soon carry them into space in America's first manned spaceflights. *Top row, from left to right:* Alan B. Shepard, Walter "Wally" Schirra, and John H. Glenn Jr. *Bottom row, from left to right:* Virgil "Gus" Grissom, M. Scott Carpenter, Donald K. "Deke" Slayton, and L. Gordon Cooper Jr.

space, perform a series of tasks, and return safely, with no ill effects. After Kennedy issued his challenge to NASA and the nation at large, the space agency worked quickly to create two new programs. The first, Gemini, was intended to solve all the technical problems involved in sending human beings the 240,000 miles (386,243 km) from Earth to the Moon. The goal of the second program, Apollo, was to actually land astronauts

MAKING THE GRADE

The requirements for the second group of NASA astronauts were few but difficult to fulfill. An applicant had to have been a civilian or military test pilot for high-performance aircraft. He had to have a degree in science or engineering. The age limit was thirty-five. Finally, an astronaut could not be taller than six feet because he had to be able to fit in a fairly small space capsule.

Neil Armstrong met all of these requirements, as did more than 200 other men. They were all put through a grueling five-day physical exam and a series of equally exhausting psychological tests. The results of these tests whittled the list down to thirty-two candidates. Another round of physical and psychological examinations followed, as well as tests of technical knowledge. By September, nine astronauts had made the final cut, including Neil Armstrong. The Nine, as they came to be called, joined the Original Seven—the Mercury astronauts—in preparing to journey to the Moon.

on the Moon and allow them to walk on its surface. To staff the Gemini and Apollo missions, a new group of astronauts had to be recruited and trained. Neil Armstrong would be included in their ranks.

General Training

Preparation for a spaceflight had three main parts: general training, development of equipment and systems for the specific mission, and testing every single human, mechanical, electrical, and procedural element that would come into play during the mission. General training for the Nine was not as difficult as it had been for the Mercury 7 astronauts. The first astronauts had been operating in uncharted territory; no one knew what being in space would do to their bodies. So they had to undergo testing for every possible stress and strain, no matter how unlikely. By the time the second group of astronauts was selected, NASA had a much more complete understanding of how to adequately prepare the new astronauts for the challenges of space travel.

NASA astronaut David R. Scott receives zero gravity training aboard a C-135 air force cargo plane in 1966. Dressed in a full space suit and floating in temporary weightless conditions, Scott practices space walk techniques he will use on a later, actual spaceflight.

Weightlessness

One thing the astronauts were certain to experience in space was weightlessness, also called zero-G (for zero gravity). They would not simply be riding to the Moon as passive passengers. Instead, they would be performing tasks during their spaceflights, so they had to be able to function in the weightlessness of space. The astronaut training program had developed a way to simulate zero gravity in Earth's atmosphere: the zero-G plane.

The zero-G plane was an air force KC-135 (similar to a Boeing 707). The seats were removed and the cabin was padded, so the astronauts would not get hurt as they were learning to adjust to floating freely in space. The plane would soar through the sky in a steep arc, generating two to three Gs. As it reached its highest point of altitude, it nosed down and began a steep but controlled descent. For twenty to thirty seconds, as the plane was cresting at and beginning to descend from its highest altitude, a momentary sense of weightlessness was created. This is similar to the feeling you get in your stomach when a car crests a hill at high speed or a roller coaster begins a sharp decline. Your whole body lifts out of the seat and your stomach feels as if it is rising to your throat. The plane would make thirty to forty of these maneuvers in a single flight. The KC-135, which is still used by NASA for weightlessness training, is nicknamed the "vomit comet" for the effect it has on many trainees' stomachs. Despite nausea, astronauts must learn to work in this environment.

Twenty-second spurts of weightlessness in the zero-G plane were enough to practice some basic tasks. In space, however, astronauts would experience weightlessness for hours or days. To simulate longer periods of weightlessness, the astronauts used underwater training. They were submerged in a deep tank, and weights were attached to various parts of their bodies. The water would lift them up and the weights would pull them down to closely simulate the reduced gravity of the Moon's surface. As they floated underwater, astronauts practiced the more complicated, time-consuming tasks they would need to complete during their missions.

Centrifuge

Even the ordeal of the dreaded vomit comet was easy compared to what Neil Armstrong and the others called "the wheel." It was a giant centrifuge—a capsule attached to the end of a 50-foot (15.24-m) arm that whirled in circles at an extremely high speed. The purpose of the wheel was to simulate the crushing, stressful G forces of launch and reentry. As the astronauts were spun in

This is the centrifuge located in the Flight Acceleration Facility at the Manned Spacecraft Center in Houston, Texas. The 50-foot (15.24-m) arm can swing the three-man capsule attached to it at speeds that simulate the G forces of a spaceflight's launch and reentry.

the device, the pressure pushed them against the wall of the capsule (this is known as centrifugal force). When the force reached five Gs, they began to have difficulty breathing. At eight Gs, they could not move their arms. At twelve, they could no longer see. The limit for both man and machine was fifteen Gs.

In the spring of 1963, NASA's astronauts participated in tropic survival training for a few days at Albrook Air Force Base in Panama. From left to right are an unidentified trainer, Neil Armstrong, John Glenn, L. Gordon Cooper, and Pete Conrad.

Survival Training

While Armstrong was mastering the physical aspects of space travel and weightlessness, he also had to prepare for what might come after reentry and splashdown back on planet Earth. The spacecraft were all programmed to land in the ocean. Armstrong and his fellow astronauts had to practice egress—getting out of their spaceship after its return to Earth.

For practice, they were dropped in sealed capsules into the waters of the Gulf of Mexico. They had to unfasten their harnesses, open the door of the capsule, swim to the surface of the water, inflate life rafts, and climb into them. In case they landed off course, far from rescue vessels, they had to practice staying afloat in rough weather and high seas and learn how to make saltwater drinkable. They also had to be prepared for landing on ground, in case something went very wrong during reentry and threw them far off course. Armstrong was left in jungles in Panama and in deserts in Nevada so that he would learn how to survive in remote places until help arrived. He became experienced in eating whatever he could find in the environment around him and sleeping in whatever shelter he could make out of nearby materials.

As interesting as it may have been to figure out which desert snake was good to eat, Armstrong was eager to complete this training and get assigned to a specific spaceflight. That day finally came in February 1965. Neil Armstrong was assigned to a Gemini mission.

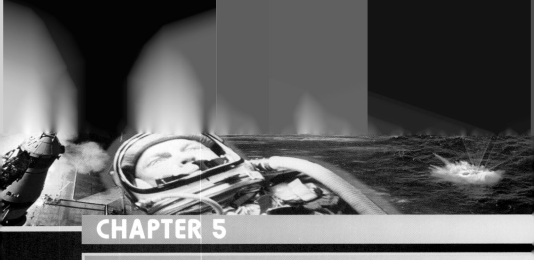

CHAPTER 5

INTO SPACE

The first space program to which Neil Armstrong was assigned was named for the third constellation of the zodiac. The constellation was called Gemini, the Greek word for "twins," because of its two bright stars, Castor and Pollux. The Gemini spacecraft would each hold two astronauts (the Mercury capsules were piloted solo).

The Gemini program was developed in January 1962, after President Kennedy challenged NASA to put a man on the Moon and bring him back safely before the 1960s ended. To get to the Moon, man and machine would have to be able to stay in space for as long as two weeks. At least two astronauts would have to participate in the mission—one to pilot the vehicle that would land on the Moon and the other to stay behind and maintain control of the craft that would take them back to Earth after the lunar landing was completed. A way of separating those two spacecraft for the Moon landing and reuniting them for the trip home would have to be created. It was a challenging task, but it was one Armstrong was excited to undertake.

Preparation

The task was so big and involved so many details that the work had to be divided among all the astronauts. A year after Armstrong was accepted into NASA, fourteen astronauts were added to help shoulder the workload. Some designed navigation systems or worked on communications or environmental control (the control of things like oxygen levels and cabin temperature). Others specialized in flight suits, cockpit design, recovery systems, and thousands of other pieces that made up the giant puzzle of spaceflight. Armstrong was assigned to

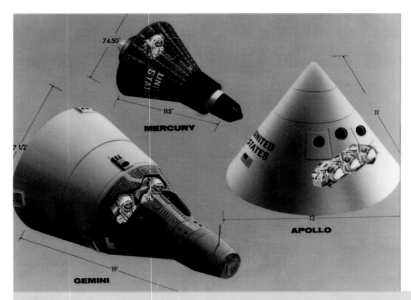

This illustration shows the Mercury, Gemini, and Apollo spacecraft, their dimensions, and their size relative to each other. Cutaway views reveal how many astronauts could fit into each capsule. They also give a good sense of just how cramped the capsules were, even the relatively roomy, three-person Apollo craft.

design trainers and simulators, the same kind of work he had performed for seven years at Edwards Air Force Base with NACA.

In addition to his specific responsibilities, Armstrong spent hundreds of hours in briefings. These were lectures about how the different parts of the craft and the mission worked. Systems briefings described the computers, the guidance system, the engine valves, and all the other "bells and whistles" that make the ship fly. Operational briefings explained who would do what and when.

These activities and the ongoing physical training took place at different locations. Parts of the spacecraft were being built at NASA's mission control center in Houston, while other parts were being constructed at Cape Canaveral in Florida (renamed Cape Kennedy following the president's assassination in 1963), where the spacecraft would be launched. Additional spacecraft parts were being built at the McDonnell manufacturing plant in St. Louis, Missouri. Centrifuge training took place in Johnsville, Pennsylvania.

Whenever Armstrong had to travel to one of these cities, he flew there himself. NASA kept a fleet of T-33s and T-38s—air force training jets—for just this purpose. Taking the jets on the frequent trips between the various sites was not only fast and convenient, but it also kept the astronauts' piloting skills sharp. Even though floating through the zero gravity of space was not very similar to flying through clouds at three or four Gs, both

NASA SIMULATORS

The ability to react and make snap decisions was further tested in the simulators Armstrong helped design. The simulators were mock-ups of the actual spaceships. In them, the instruments looked, felt, and performed exactly like the real thing. The mission controllers used the simulators to prepare the astronauts for every emergency imaginable. They dropped the spacecraft's speed suddenly, raised its angle, and changed cabin temperatures. They made levers stick and instruments malfunction. They "drove" the spaceships through meteor belts and radiation fields. Although other astronauts accused the controllers of creating ridiculous scenarios that would never happen in real life, Armstrong did not complain. He liked the challenges posed by the controllers and enjoyed the split-second problem solving they required. He also wanted to be prepared for anything and everything he might encounter on his way to the Moon.

experiences could require quick reactions and split-second decision making.

First Mission

Neil Armstrong was in the astronaut program for three years before finally being assigned to a mission. When the assignment came, it was not what he had long hoped for and expected. He was to be backup commander for *Gemini 5*, meaning that he would remain on the ground during his first mission. Later he said in an interview with Stephen Ambrose and Douglas Brinkley that he was "really pleased to be assigned to a flight and quite satisfied to be in that [backup] position." He said he would have been happy doing anything that took the United States farther into space and closer to the Moon, even if that meant staying behind to provide support to his fellow astronauts who were lucky enough to be rocketing far beyond Earth's atmosphere. The pressure was on to complete the tasks of the Gemini program and get on with the Moon landings of Apollo. It was already 1965; half the decade was gone and Kennedy's challenge had still not been met.

Even though it was unlikely that Armstrong would serve as commander of *Gemini 5*, he had to prepare as though he would. He spent most of his waking hours focused on the mission. The team of four men—two crew and two backup—were together almost constantly for the six months it took to get ready for the flight. They spent very little time at home with their families, instead traveling between St. Louis, Houston, and Cape Canaveral. All four put in long, exhausting hours, sometimes having to perform tests at two o'clock in the morning.

They were rewarded for their hard work. *Gemini 5* was a success and went off without a hitch. Thankfully, none of the emergencies for which the crew had practiced so hard ever arose. Armstrong, in particular, received the supreme award for his excellent service. He was assigned to the prime crew of *Gemini 8*. This meant that he would finally be going into space.

Gemini 8

By the time Neil Armstrong climbed into the cockpit of a real spaceship, the Gemini program had already made giant leaps toward the goal of a

This is a photograph of the *Gemini 8* prime and backup crews. The prime crew, David R. Scott *(left)* and Neil Armstrong, sit with a model of the Gemini capsule between them. Standing behind them is the backup crew of Richard F. Gordon Jr. *(left)* and Charles Conrad Jr.

lunar landing. In *Gemini 3*, Virgil "Gus" Grissom and John Young proved that astronauts could use hand controls to maneuver a spacecraft, steering it where they wanted it to go. The ability to move spacecraft into a specific position would be critical when astronauts who had landed on the Moon had to orchestrate a rendezvous (meeting) of their lunar module with the command module orbiting over the lunar surface. If the two craft did not meet and dock (attach together) properly, the astronauts would be stranded in space, unable to return home.

During *Gemini 4*, Ed White exited his spaceship and spacewalked (floated outside the craft while attached to it with a long tether) for twenty-one minutes, testing his ability to work in

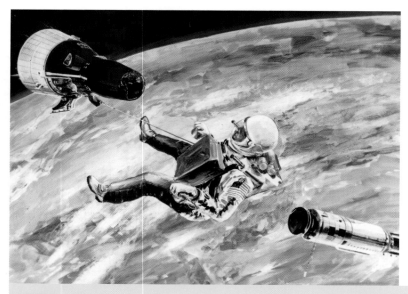

In this artist's drawing, a Gemini astronaut is engaged in an extra vehicular activity (EVA), or a space walk. The tether secures the astronaut to the Gemini spacecraft in the upper left corner. In the lower right corner is the Agena target vehicle, which helped Gemini astronauts test rendezvous and docking techniques.

space outside a vehicle, just as astronauts would have to do on the lunar surface. *Gemini 5*, on which Armstrong worked so hard, showed that humans would have no trouble staying in space for at least eight days, simulating the length of time necessary for a round-trip journey to the Moon. *Gemini 7* pushed that limit to two weeks. The *Gemini 6* astronauts demonstrated that rendezvous was possible—two spacecraft were steered close together as if they were about to dock.

The task of *Gemini 8* was to dock two vehicles, as the command and lunar modules of a lunar landing mission would have to do before returning to Earth. One vehicle was an Agena rocket. This would be launched into orbit before the *Gemini 8* capsule. It had a cone-shaped collar at one end that was fitted to receive the Gemini spacecraft, which would be launched into orbit forty-one minutes after the rocket. This Gemini module would be carrying Neil Armstrong and Dave Scott. Armstrong's job was to catch up with the Agena rocket and steer the nose of the module into the target vehicle's docking collar. Then Scott was to space-walk outside the spacecraft for two and a half hours, performing various tasks. After three days, the vehicles would undock and the two astronauts would return to Earth.

That was the plan, and it began with a flawless launch on March 16, 1966. From an altitude few other humans had ever reached before or since, Armstrong spotted the Hawaiian Islands through the clouds. He passed over California and marveled at how many ships he could see near Los Angeles. Then he saw Rogers Dry Lake, where he landed X-15s just four years earlier. Soon the planet slipped from view, and the crew began its work.

After *Gemini 8* circled Earth once, the two-man team began placing it in exactly the same orbit as the Agena. Armstrong worked the controls, and Scott watched the computer readings. They orbited Earth again, confident that they were getting close to the target vehicle. During their third orbit, they detected it on their radar. The fourth time around, they spotted a pinprick of light. As they got closer, the light grew brighter. Armstrong slowed his craft to a speed of 3 inches (7.6 centimeters) per second as he delicately guided it into position. Finally he announced, "We are docked! It's really a smoothie."

The *Gemini 8* spacecraft is launched from the Kennedy Space Center at 11:41 AM on March 16, 1966, with Neil Armstrong and David Scott on board. The mission, designed to test rendezvous and docking procedures, would develop serious mechanical problems and would have to be ended early. It would still be considered a successful test of the docking procedures necessary for a Moon landing, however.

A Third Close Call

The flight continued smoothly for half an hour. But soon a serious problem arose. The connected vehicles started to roll. By that time, Armstrong and Scott had circled to the dark side of Earth—the side facing away from the Sun—and were out of radio contact with mission control. Armstrong shut down the Agena's controls and used Gemini's systems to stabilize their position. It worked for four minutes, but then the ships began spinning around and around again.

The situation was unlike any of the emergencies they had encountered in training. None of the NASA technicians and engineers at the Earth stations knew what was wrong. The astronauts were completely on their own. They flipped switches on and off, but the tumbling continued, faster and faster. They were getting dizzy and were afraid they might black out. It was time for that split-second decision making bred into fighter pilots.

Armstrong and Scott decided the problem must be in the Agena and they should undock from it. This was not an easy decision. With the

Neil Armstrong makes final adjustments and checks to the *Gemini 8* spacecraft during the pre-launch countdown. After a launch delay, *Gemini 8* finally got off the ground and managed to dock with the Gemini Agena target vehicle six and a half hours later.

vehicles spinning out of control, there was no telling what direction each would take once separated. The two craft might collide, but there seemed to be no other choice. Armstrong steadied the Gemini capsule as well as he could, then ordered Scott to hit the undocking button. When the capsule pushed away from the Agena, it spun even faster, about one revolution per second.

In this photograph taken from the *Gemini 8* capsule, the Agena docking vehicle can be seen as the two spacecraft draw closer to each other. The blurry object in the lower left of the photo is *Gemini 8*. At this point, the craft were about 2 feet (0.6 m) away from each other.

The problem was not in the Agena, but in the Gemini capsule!

The astronauts' only hope at this point was to abort the mission and try to bring their vessel out of orbit before they lost consciousness. With his vision blurring, Armstrong turned off the regular control system and turned on the reentry control system. This was not an easy decision either. It meant returning to Earth two days early and leaving many important tasks undone, such as Scott's space walk, for which he had spent hundreds of hours training. Worst of all, it meant a delay for the Moon landing program. Aside from these disappointments, however, aborting the mission also meant saving the spacecraft and preserving their own lives. These were by far the more important considerations.

Once the decision was made to abort and their capsule was again under control, Armstrong discovered what had been wrong. A switch to the number eight thruster (one of the small rocket engines attached to the capsule) had short-circuited and stuck in the "on" position. The thruster was firing

NASA engineers from mission control monitor events during the *Gemini 8* spaceflight on March 16, 1966. They were the ones who had to make the final decision about cutting the spaceflight short in the interests of astronaut and spacecraft safety. Mission control is located at the Johnson Space Center in Houston, Texas.

At top, astronauts David Scott *(left)* and Neil Armstrong *(right)* stand on the deck of the USS *Mason* as it arrives in Nahs, Okinawa, Japan. The *Mason* had recovered both the craft and crew of *Gemini 8* following its earlier-than-expected splashdown in the Pacific Ocean on March 16, 1966. At bottom, the *Gemini 8* spacecraft is hoisted aboard the *Mason*.

continuously, sending the capsule into a fast spin. He wanted to fix the problem then and there and continue with the mission. Mission rules stated, however, that when the reentry control system was activated, the trip was over. Besides, the difficult maneuverings performed while trying to regain control of the spacecraft had used up much of its fuel. So, less than eleven hours after liftoff, *Gemini 8* splashed down in the Pacific Ocean.

Armstrong was disappointed with the mission's outcome, but he was also excited. The mission had achieved its primary goal: a successful rendezvous and docking. With this achievement, the United States had gained its first lead over the Soviet Union in the space race. Perhaps most important, *Gemini 8* had tested the ability of America's astronauts and equipment to perform under extreme physical, mechanical, and mental pressure. They had passed the test with flying colors.

Immediately after Neil Armstrong's feet were back on the ground, he was ready and eager for another assignment.

CHAPTER 6

TO THE MOON

The Gemini program was designed to test all the equipment and procedures necessary to land astronauts on the Moon. The actual Moon landings would occur during the Apollo missions. Apollo was the program that succeeded Mercury and Gemini and was built upon their discoveries and achievements.

The Apollo program was designed as a step-by-step process. The first step—the A and B missions—would consist of unmanned tests of the launchers and spacecraft. The C missions would be manned tests of the command service module

(CSM)—the primary spaceship—in orbit around Earth. The lunar module (LM), the smaller craft that would detach from the CSM and land on the Moon, was to be added for the D and E missions. The F mission would reach and orbit the Moon, a dress rehearsal for an actual lunar landing, which would occur on the G mission. As a series of experiments and spaceflights provided NASA with new information, however, the plan and schedule were constantly being adjusted.

NASA now had barely three years to meet its end-of-the-decade deadline to reach the Moon. In this three-year period, not only did NASA have to design a reliable and safe command module, it also had to perfect a crucial element of any planned Moon landing—the lunar module. This was a totally new type of craft, built not for soaring through space or floating in orbit, but for departing from and returning to the command module and touching down upon and taking off from the lunar surface. In order to practice maneuvering this unique vehicle on Earth, a lunar landing research vehicle (LLRV) was built. It looked like a giant metal insect, with a boxy body and four long skinny legs. It was so tiny and cramped that it could barely hold two astronauts, who had to stand in it to operate its controls.

New Assignments

The Apollo schedule called for a D mission in late 1968—an Earth orbit that would include the lunar module. The lunar module was simply not ready, however, and in only a year the decade would come to an end and NASA's deadline to reach the Moon would pass. So, in a bold move, mission planners decided to push the lunar orbit flight ahead in the schedule. They would practice orbiting the Moon without the lunar landing module along for the trip. As a result, *Apollo 8*, an E mission, was now slated for December. Armstrong was assigned to its backup crew.

Apollo 8 electrified the country. Three men— Frank Borman, James Lovell, and William Anders—actually reached lunar orbit, circling the Moon ten times. Theirs were the first human eyes to see the far side of the Moon. They took pictures and broadcast them live to a television audience of

Apollo 8 was the first mission to take humans to the Moon and back, though it did not actually land astronauts on the Moon's surface. In this still print taken from film shot during the mission, the command module pilot, James A. Lovell Jr., is seen working some of the spacecraft's controls.

almost a billion people. In a dramatic Christmas Eve message beamed a distance of 240,000 miles (386,243 km), they read the first ten verses of the Bible. Having proved that the Apollo spacecraft could travel as far as the Moon and back, they splashed to a perfect landing in the Pacific Ocean.

For Neil Armstrong, the most exciting event of that historic six-day flight occurred behind the scenes, while *Apollo 8* was still in the sky. The NASA official who assembled the crews for all the flights called Armstrong into his office. He was making assignments for the next three missions and was asking Armstrong about *Apollo 11*. It was to be the G mission, the one that would finally land a man on the Moon. Was Armstrong interested in being a crew member of *Apollo 11*?

Neil Armstrong was more than interested; he was thrilled. This was the assignment every NASA astronaut craved. He accepted the offer without hesitation.

Preparation

Armstrong was named commander of *Apollo 11*. His crew members were Buzz Aldrin and Michael Collins. Aldrin's job was to manage the rendezvous between the command and lunar modules and all the related systems. Collins was in charge of the command module. He was to navigate Apollo to the Moon, keep it in orbit while Armstrong and Aldrin descended to the Moon, and steer it back to Earth after the lunar landing was completed and

This 1969 portrait shows the prime crew of the *Apollo 11* lunar landing mission. From left to right, they are Neil Armstrong, commander; Michael Collins, command module pilot; and Edwin E. "Buzz" Aldrin Jr., lunar module pilot. Collins remained in orbit overhead while Armstrong and Aldrin descended to the Moon and explored the lunar surface.

the two crafts had rendezvoused and docked. Armstrong's responsibility was to fly the lunar module to the Moon's surface. The three astronauts had about six months to prepare for the biggest trip of their lives.

By far, the majority of the mission preparation was spent in flight simulations. For Armstrong, that meant flying mock-ups of the lunar module as well as spending many long hours in a flight simulator that never left the ground. The simulator's computers, directed by mission control engineers, would create a variety of lifelike situations to which the astronauts would have to respond. In one of these simulator tests, Armstrong and Aldrin were smoothly guiding the lunar module toward a simulated Moon,

Neil Armstrong participates in simulation training in 1969 to prepare for the *Apollo 11* lunar landing mission. The training took place in the Kennedy Space Center's Flight Crew Training Building. He is standing in a mock-up of the lunar module that he and Buzz Aldrin would soon pilot to the Moon's surface.

just as they had successfully done hundreds of times before. Armstrong was at the controls, and Aldrin was giving him readings from the various gauges. Without any warning, the lunar module suddenly began to roll. Through their capsule "windows"— actually TV screens—the astronauts could see the Moon tilt wildly. The problem that had occurred on Armstrong's *Gemini 8* flight was happening again here: a thruster was stuck in the "on" position. With the thruster stuck and continuously firing, the lunar module would slam into the Moon's surface and the men would surely be "killed."

Aldrin continued to call out the readings to Armstrong. He was growing more frantic but did not want to tell his commander what to do. According to Choikin's *A Man on the Moon*, Aldrin became sure that they would crash if they did not do something drastic immediately. He growled, "Neil, hit abort!" The mission controllers agreed: "*Apollo 11*, we recommend you abort." Armstrong, however, was determined to solve the problem and salvage the mission, but this was no longer possible. Within seconds, all the gauges stopped moving and the picture of the Moon on the TV screen window froze in place. If

SAYING NO TO
THE PRESIDENT

Mission controllers took great care that nothing would endanger the *Apollo 11* mission. They worried that the astronauts might get sick, which would delay or postpone the launch. So for the three weeks before launch, Armstrong, Aldrin, and Collins were placed in medical quarantine. They spent their time in simulators and in their living quarters but away from the general public. When reporters were allowed to interview them, they and the astronauts wore masks. President Richard Nixon wanted to have dinner with the crew the night before the flight, but NASA would not permit it. The president's germs might make them sick!

this had been a real spaceflight instead of a simulated one, the mission would be a tragic failure and the astronauts would lie dead on the lunar surface, surrounded by the wreckage of their lunar module.

As dramatic and vivid as it was, a simulator failure did not bother Armstrong. He believed that the purpose of the simulator was to allow the astronauts to find the limits of their and the craft's abilities. If he never pushed himself further than he thought he could go, how would he know where those limits were? Even a failed test provided valuable information, and a simulator was a safe place for testing. After the simulated crash, Armstrong felt even more prepared for and confident about the real thing.

The Flight Plan

The launch of *Apollo 11* was scheduled for July 16, 1969. The plan was as follows:

1. A Saturn rocket would carry the CSM *Columbia* and the LM *Eagle* from Cape Kennedy and put them in Earth orbit in eleven minutes.

2. The Saturn rocket would then be reignited, hurling the spacecraft out of Earth orbit and toward the Moon. As they traveled to the Moon, the crew would send color television images back to Earth.

3. On the third day of the mission, *Columbia* would separate from the *Saturn* rocket and turn 180 degrees. Within the rocket's frame was stored the lunar module *Eagle*. *Columbia* would dock with the lunar module and pull it away from the spent rocket.

4. The crew would slow the craft down to just the right speed so it could be "caught" by the Moon's gravity and be held in lunar orbit. It would go around the Moon thirteen times. On the second orbit, TV pictures of the lunar surface would be transmitted to Earth.

5. On July 20, Armstrong and Aldrin would enter the *Eagle*, separate it from *Columbia*, and land it on the Moon's Sea of Tranquility—a broad plain in the northern hemisphere of the Moon.

6. Armstrong and Aldrin would exit from the *Eagle*, walk on the Moon, take pictures, and collect samples of rocks.

7. Back in the *Eagle*, Armstrong would initiate liftoff and pilot the lunar module to a rendezvous and docking with *Columbia*.

8. With only one rocket remaining on the spacecraft, the three astronauts would make the three-day trip back to Earth and splash down in the Pacific Ocean. For the entire eight days, the crew would be in constant communication with controllers at the Manned Spacecraft Center in Houston, Texas.

From the very beginning, *Apollo 11* went almost exactly according to plan. July 16, 1969, was a beautiful day, and the liftoff was flawless. As the world watched on television, Jan Armstrong witnessed her husband's history-making launch from a boat in the Banana River, as close to the Cape as she could get. Her sons were with her—Ricky, then twelve, and Mark, who was six. The boys were excited. "My

As the *Apollo 11* prelaunch countdown gets under way on July 16, 1969, astronauts Neil Armstrong, Michael Collins, and Buzz Aldrin Jr. exit the Kennedy Space Center's Manned Spacecraft Operations Building, where they have been suited up.

daddy's going to the Moon," Mark is quoted as saying in *First on the Moon.* "It will take him three days to get there. I want to go to the Moon some-day with my daddy." In a way, Mark and millions of other people did go to the Moon with his father. The live television and radio transmissions gave audiences on Earth a very good idea of what was happening 240,000 miles (386,243 km) above them.

The Landing

This fantastic journey amazed even the highly trained, experienced crew. Armstrong, who was ordinarily calm and matter-of-fact, sounded

The Saturn V rocket that will help carry Neil Armstrong, Buzz Aldrin, and Michael Collins to the Moon lifts off on July 16, 1969. Armstrong and Aldrin would become the first humans ever to set foot on the lunar surface. In doing so, they fulfilled President John F. Kennedy's dream of landing an American on the Moon before the end of the 1960s.

excited when he got his first glimpse of the Moon. He had seen pictures of it brought back from previous Apollo flights, but this, he said in *First on the Moon,* was "like the difference between watching a real football game and watching it on TV—no substitute for actually being here."

When the time came for Armstrong and Aldrin to climb into the lunar module and separate it from the command module, the two vehicles were on the dark side of the Moon and out of radio contact with Earth. The controllers in Houston held their breath. "How does it look?" mission control asked anxiously when the astronauts reemerged on the Moon's near side. Finally Armstrong announced, "The *Eagle* has wings." Now *Eagle* and *Columbia* were separated, each circling the Moon in its own orbit. After checking all the instruments, the controllers gave Armstrong the go-ahead to begin the descent to the lunar surface.

Not long into the descent, an alarm began to go off. The alarm code was 1202, and neither Armstrong nor Aldrin knew what that meant. Should they abort and try to return to lunar orbit? They radioed mission control, and someone there

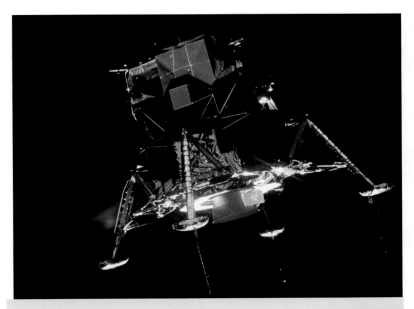

The *Apollo 11* lunar module, the *Eagle*, descends to the surface of the Moon. This photograph was taken from the command module, *Columbia*, on July 20, 1969. Because of unexpected difficulties in finding a safe place to land, the *Eagle* would touch down with only half a minute's worth of fuel remaining.

recognized the alarm code as serious. The code meant that the computer that controlled much of the descent and the landing was overloaded. At any minute, it could shut down. The alarm suddenly stopped, and Houston said all was probably well. The mission was still a go.

Just when calm seemed to be restored, however, the alarm went off again. The controllers shifted

The staff of mission control watch video images of Neil Armstrong and Buzz Aldrin as they take their first steps on the Moon on July 20, 1969.

some of the workload of the lunar module's computer to one at mission control, and the alarm again stopped. The mission was still a go.

Then a different alarm sounded. When it stopped, another one went off. Frantic controllers, with only seconds to decide how safe the situation was, continued to give the go command. Later, when asked how he was able to remain so calm and single-minded under such intense pressure, Armstrong said, "During simulations we were programmed to abort; on the actual mission we were programmed to land" (as quoted in Reginald Turnill's *The Moonlandings*). Armstrong simply ignored the alarms and focused on landing the craft. When he was 1,100 feet (335 m) from the lunar surface, he could see that the computer was piloting the craft into a crater surrounded by boulders as big as small cars. He grabbed the controls, overrode the computer, and slowed the descent to keep from crashing on the rocks. He barely skimmed past the boulders at an altitude of only 350 feet (107 m).

Back in Houston, the controllers did not know what was going on. They knew only that alarms were blaring, that the *Eagle* had slowed down, and that it was not obeying its computers. They could only hope that Armstrong was piloting it and that he could get it down safely.

Armstrong was indeed piloting the lunar module, but he was having trouble finding a safe spot for landing. Dangerous and jagged rocks and craters were everywhere, and the search for a relatively smooth, flat landing area used up much of the module's fuel. Finally, only 100 feet (30 m) above the lunar surface, Armstrong spotted a level place and headed for it. By the time the lunar module's legs touched down, it had only twenty seconds worth of descent fuel left (there was a separate fuel tank for the ascent back to the command module).

Armstrong hit the engine stop button, and for a moment all was incredibly silent after the tense minutes of a whining engine, the anxious chatter of

mission control, and the screaming alarms. The two astronauts could finally relax, and they grinned in disbelief and wonder. Then for all the world to hear, Armstrong announced into his radio microphone, "Houston, Tranquility Base here. The *Eagle* has landed." Mission control erupted in joyous relief and celebration. "Roger, Tranquility, we copy you on the ground," a controller replied. "You got a bunch of guys about to turn blue. We're breathing again."

Exploring the Moon

Now that everyone was breathing more easily, Armstrong and Aldrin were eager to get out of their cramped quarters and start exploring the Moon. Originally they were scheduled to take a four-hour nap after landing, just in case some emergency occurred later in the mission and they needed to be at full strength and alertness. But who could sleep in this brand-new, exotic world? They completed the necessary checks of all the lunar module's systems, then prepared to exit the *Eagle* without a nap.

With a camera mounted on the outside of the *Eagle* running, the astronauts opened the module's hatch. Armstrong's boots and legs appeared on millions of TV screens on Earth. Then his body and arms came into view as he backed down the steps of the lunar module. "I'm at the foot of the ladder," he informed the waiting world. "I'm going to step off the LM now."

For months, people had wondered what Armstrong

Neil Armstrong, standing in the lunar module, smiles for the camera during the lunar landing mission. He was about to become the first human being ever to set foot on the Moon's surface.

would say when he became the first human being to set foot on the Moon. Lots of people had offered him suggestions. Armstrong himself did not actually decide on his historic words until he was ready to step down. The words he chose echoed his conviction that this historic moment was not the achievement of any one person or of a single country, but an amazing opportunity and triumph for all people. As he leapt off the ladder onto the lunar surface, he said, "That's one small step for man, one giant leap for mankind."

Armstrong was pleased to discover that stepping on the Moon was much easier than he had expected. The force of gravity was only one-sixth of that experienced on Earth, and yet it felt almost normal. Perhaps this was due to all the weightless training performed underwater and in the KC-135. Within minutes, Aldrin joined him on the lunar surface. Together they unveiled a plaque and mounted it on one of the legs of the lunar module. It was signed by all three crew members and President Nixon. Armstrong read it for his radio and television audience: "Here men from the planet Earth first set foot upon the Moon July 1969, A.D. We came in peace for all mankind."

The giant leap and the plaque may have proclaimed that the Moon landing was for all mankind, but the mission was achieved and paid for by the United States, and its long competition with the Soviets required some patriotic gesture. The world's first lunar explorers had brought an American flag to place on the Moon. It would never flap and flutter like flags do on Earth because the Moon has no wind. To keep the flag from drooping straight down for millions of years,

Above is one of the few photos of Neil Armstrong on his historic first moonwalk. Astronaut Buzz Aldrin took the photo with a 70mm camera. The inset photo shows the plaque that the astronauts left behind on the Moon. It states: "Here men from the planet Earth first set foot upon the Moon July 1969, A.D. We came in peace for all mankind."

the astronauts had put a metal strip along the banner's upper edge, keeping it extended rigidly. When it was all set up, Aldrin stood back and saluted it while Armstrong snapped his picture. Armstrong took lots of pictures. Because he had the camera most of the time, there are very few

Buzz Aldrin is seen here setting up experiment packages near the lunar module. The astronauts spent two hours and thirty-two minutes outside the lunar module on the Moon's surface. While outside, they conducted several experiments and collected 46 pounds (21 kilograms) of Moon rocks and soil samples to take back to Earth.

pictures of Armstrong on the Moon. His image, however, is occasionally reflected in the visor of Buzz Aldrin's spacesuit.

The two men had far more work to do than simply taking pictures, but they had less than three hours' worth of oxygen. So they set out exploring the lunar surface, reporting back to mission control and collecting samples of Moon rocks. By the time they climbed back into the lunar module, stowed their lunar soil samples, and prepared the LM for the next day's departure from the Moon, they had been awake for more than twenty-four hours. They tried to sleep as best they could in the tiny module that was not built for comfort. They would need all their energy for the next day. With their mission on the Moon accomplished, they would face the difficult task of taking off from the lunar surface, meeting and docking with *Columbia*, and beginning the journey back to Earth.

BACK ON EARTH

The return to *Columbia* and Earth was smooth sailing all the way. On the way back down through Earth's atmosphere, Neil Armstrong thought about the crowds of people who would be asking for interviews, handshakes, and autographs. He disliked crowds, and he hated attention. Although he knew that he was the public face and voice of this mission, he was only one small part of its success. He wished everyone would focus on someone else. In the crew's final telecast from space, he tried to redirect public attention from him and toward others equally deserving: "The responsibility for this flight lies first with history and with the

A ticker-tape parade was held for the returned *Apollo 11* astronauts in New York City on August 13, 1969. It was said to have been the largest ticker-tape parade ever. Pictured in the lead car, seated high in the back seat, are, from left, Buzz Aldrin, Michael Collins, and Neil Armstrong.

giants of science who have preceded this effort. Next, with the American people . . . four administrations and their Congresses . . . the agency and industry teams that build our spacecraft . . . To these people, tonight, we give a special thank you" (as quoted in *First on the Moon*).

New Assignments

Though only just returned to Earth from the Moon, the *Apollo 11* astronauts were already eager for a new mission. Their next assignment, however, was not in space. It was not even in the field of astronautics or engineering. It was a political duty that is the burden of all national heroes: public relations. The *Apollo 11* astronauts were now thrust into the role of spokespeople for the United States and for the American space program. They gave interviews and news conferences and met with leaders of many nations. There seemed no end to the parties, parades, dinners, awards ceremonies, and other events honoring their accomplishments. They were sent on a world tour, visiting twenty-three countries in thirty-eight days.

Armstrong would rather have been sitting in a simulator in Houston than around a table at a fancy dinner party. He would have preferred to be sent back into space rather than on a world tour. Still, he smiled, waved, and represented his country well. All the while, though, he was itching to get back in the air, back to what he loved doing.

Other astronauts, however, were waiting their turn to fly the remaining Apollo missions. Armstrong

Neil Armstrong delivers a speech to a joint session of Congress on September 16, 1969. A speech delivered to the combined representatives of the House and Senate is an honor usually reserved for the president and other world leaders. In the background sit Vice President Spiro T. Agnew *(left)* and the House Speaker, John McCormack *(right)*.

had been given a fantastic adventure, and those who had helped make it happen now wanted their shot at the same dream. *Apollo 11* was to be Armstrong's last spaceflight.

Soon after *Apollo 11*, a NASA administrator asked Armstrong for his help. The space agency had two focuses: aeronautics and astronautics. Aeronautics is the science and art of flight within Earth's atmosphere, and astronautics is the science of spaceflight, of flying beyond Earth's atmosphere. Armstrong now had extensive experience in both. The NASA administrator asked him to leave the astronaut corps and work instead as deputy associate administrator for aeronautics.

As Armstrong considered the offer, he thought about where he could make the greater contribution. He believed that anyone could learn how to be an astronaut, but he had aeronautics skills and knowledge that few others possessed. He accepted the aeronautics job and moved his family to Washington, D.C. Before long, however, Armstrong found his new position frustrating. It was more political than technical, and the slow pace of government decision-making kept him from getting things done. He was far too busy with persuading politicians to get behind programs and not nearly involved enough in the nuts and bolts of the programs themselves.

Back to Ohio

In the midst of this frustration, a completely different job offer came his way. Armstrong had always thought about teaching. He knew he had a wealth of knowledge and experience that he could share with others, and he loved to be around young people who wanted to learn. So when the University of Cincinnati invited him to teach aerospace engineering, he jumped at the chance to return to his home state and retire from NASA.

Armstrong spent nine years as a professor there. He bought a farm in Lebanon, just 100 miles (161 km) from the airport where he had taken flying lessons as a boy. There, he settled comfortably into a 100-year-old farmhouse. He was happy to be leading a normal life, out of the public eye, and he was delighted to be training some of the brightest young minds in the country.

Following his stint at the University of Cincinnati, Armstrong looked to see what contribution he

In 1991, Neil Armstrong, the first human being to set foot on the Moon, was inducted into the Aerospace Walk of Honor in Lancaster, California. The honor came thirty-six years after he entered the field of aeronautics with NACA and twenty-two years after his historic lunar landing. Armstrong has spent a total of eight days and fourteen hours in space.

could make to private companies that were doing creative work in aeronautics or electronics. He served on the boards of several such companies. Whatever job he held, Armstrong was always willing to use his unique talents to serve his country. While he was teaching in Cincinnati, he also served as chairman of the Presidential Advisory Committee for the Peace Corps. After that, he worked on the National

Commission on Space, helping define new goals for the space program. When the space shuttle *Challenger* exploded during takeoff in 1986, Armstrong accepted the role of vice chairman of the presidential commission that investigated the tragic accident.

Above is a close-up view of an *Apollo 11* astronaut's footprint left in the lunar soil during Neil Armstrong and Buzz Aldrin's walk on the Moon .

Of all his many achievements and accomplishments, Neil Armstrong will be most remembered as the person who made the first footprint on the Moon. He will be remembered by his fellow astronauts as a team player who always remained cool even under the greatest pressure. He will be remembered by the press as the astronaut least likely to give an interview, but the most likely to decline in a polite, respectful, and gracious manner. Finally, he will be remembered by history as the man who, while taking one small step for himself, took one giant leap for mankind.

GLOSSARY

abort To stop an action or a mission.

antiaircraft Something directed against airplanes, such as guns and missiles.

auditor A person who examines financial accounts to see that they are accurate.

command service module (CSM) The main craft on a space mission that features two modules attached together. The command module contains the crew, spacecraft operations systems, and reentry equipment. The service module carries most of the craft's supply of oxygen, water, and fuel.

corps A group of persons, a unit, or a subdivision, usually within the military.

decorated The term used to describe a person who has received medals for exceptional service in the armed forces.

G force The weight of gravity placed on a human body as it moves through space. One G is what the body feels when it is at rest on Earth. Six Gs—the force felt during many rocket takeoffs—is six times the weight of gravity experienced on Earth. Weightlessness is zero G.

lunar module (LM) The craft attached to the Apollo command module that ferried the astronauts from the command module to the Moon and back.

Mach A measure of speed. Sound travels at Mach 1. Mach 2 would be twice the speed of sound.

module An independently operable unit that is part of a larger spacecraft.

National Commission on Space A presidential committee that developed long-range goals for the national space program.

puddle jumper A small plane that flies short distances.

rocket An engine that when fired can deliver a spacecraft out of Earth's atmosphere and into space.

simulate To imitate or be like something else.

simulator A device that imitates conditions that pilots and astronauts are likely to face.

FOR MORE INFORMATION

American Astronautical Society
6352 Rolling Mill Place, Suite 102
Springfield, VA 22152-2354
Web site: http://www.astronautical.org

Jet Propulsion Laboratory
Public Services Office
Mail Stop 186-113
4800 Oak Grove Drive
Pasadena, CA 91109
Web site: http://www.jpl.nasa.gov

Johnson Space Center
Visitors Center
1601 NASA Road 1
Houston, TX 77058
Web site: http://www.jsc.nasa.gov

Kennedy Space Center Visitor Complex
Mail Code: XA/Public Inquiries
Kennedy Space Center, FL 32899
Web site: http://www.ksc.nasa.gov

NASA Headquarters
Information Center
Washington, DC 20546-0001
Web site: http://www.nasa.gov

National Air and Space Museum
7th and Independence Avenue SW
Washington, DC 20560
Web site: http://www.nasm.si.edu

Web Sites

Due to the changing nature of Internet links, the Rosen Publishing Group, Inc., has developed an online list of Web sites related to the subject of this book. This site is updated regularly. Please use this link to access the list:

http://www.rosenlinks.com/lasb/narm

FOR FURTHER READING

Aldrin, Buzz, and John Barnes. *The Return.* New York: Tor Books, 2001.

Bredeson, Carmen. *Neil Armstrong.* Berkeley Heights, NJ: Enslow Publishers, 1998.

Cole, Michael D. *Astronauts: Training for Space.* Berkeley Heights, NJ: Enslow Publishers, 1999.

Combs, Lisa M. *Rocket to the Moon: The Incredible Story of the First Lunar Landing.* Mahwah, NJ: Troll Associates, 1999.

Crocker, Chris. *Great American Astronauts.* New York: Franklin Watts, 1988.

Dunham, Montrew. *Neil Armstrong: Young Pilot.* New York: Simon & Schuster, 1996.

Ganeri, Anita. *Neil Armstrong.* North Mankato, MN: Thameside Press, 1999.

Glatzer, Jenna. *The Exploration of the Moon: How American Astronauts Traveled 240,000 Miles to the Moon and Back, and the Fascinating Things They Found There.* Vaughn, Ontario: Mason Crest Publishers, 2002.

Gold, Susan D. *Countdown to the Moon.* New York: Crestwood House, 1992.

Hayhurst, Chris. *Astronauts: Life Exploring Outer Space.* New York: The Rosen Publishing Group, Inc., 2001.

Hehner, Barbara. *First on the Moon: What It Was Like When Man Landed on the Moon.* New York: Hyperion, 1999.

Siy, Alexandra. *Footprints on the Moon.* Watertown, MA: Charlesbridge, 2001.

Stott, Carole. *Space Exploration.* New York: Dorling Kindersley Publishing, 2000.

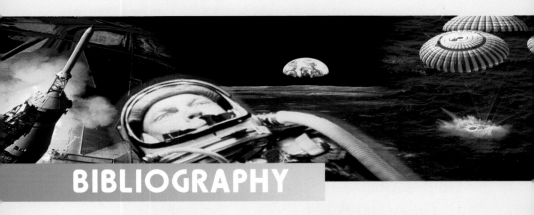

BIBLIOGRAPHY

Aldrin, Buzz, and John Barnes. *The Return*. New York: Tor Books, 2001.

Aldrin, Buzz, and Malcolm McConnell. *Men from Earth*. New York: Bantam Doubleday, 1991.

Ambrose, Stephen E., and Douglas Brinkley. *"An Interview with Neil A. Armstrong."* NASA Johnson Space Center Oral History Project. September 19, 2001. Retrieved March 2003 (http://jsc.nasa.gov/history/oral_histories/ArmstrongNA/ArmstrongNA_9-19-01.pdf).

Armstrong, Neil, Michael Collins, and Edwin E. Aldrin, Jr. *First on the Moon*. Boston: Little, Brown and Company, 1970.

Chaikin, Andrew. *A Man on the Moon: The Voyages of the Apollo Astronauts*. New York: Viking, 1994.

Collins, Michael. *Carrying the Fire*. New York: Bantam, 1983.

Godwin, Robert, ed. *Apollo 11: The NASA Mission Reports,* Volume 3. New York: Apogee Books, 2002.

Hacker, Barton C., and James M. Grimwood. *On the Shoulders of Titans: A History of Project Gemini.* Washington, DC: NASA Special Publications, 1977.

NASA. *"Apollo Flight Summaries."* March 2001. Retrieved March 2003(http://www-pao.ksc .nasa.gov/kscpao/history/apollo/ flight-summary.htm).

NASA. *"Biographies of Apollo 11 Astronauts."* 1999. Retrieved March 2003 (http://history. nasa.gov/ap11ann/astrobios.htm).

Reynolds, David, and Wally Schirra. *Apollo: The Epic Journey to the Moon.* New York: Harcourt, 2002.

Turnill, Reginald. *The Moonlandings: An Eyewitness Account.* Cambridge, UK: Cambridge University Press, 2003.

Wright, Donna Wisener. *"Despite His Celebrity, Neil Armstrong Is 'Just One of Us' in His Hometown."* Knight Ridder/Tribune News Service, July 19, 1994.

INDEX

About the Author

Ann Byers is a teacher, youth worker, thesis editor, and writer who lives in Fresno, California. Her husband and four grown children enjoy reading her books.

Photo Credits

Cover, pp. 1, 27, 37, 43, 46, 49, 50, 54, 59, 60, 63, 65, 66, 67, 68, 73, 75, 76, 82, 83, 86, 89, 91, 92, 95, 100, 101 courtesy of NASA; pp. 4–5, 23 © Corbis; pp. 7, 9, 30, 33, 35, 40, 97 © Bettmann/Corbis; p. 13 © Layne Kennedy/Corbis; p. 17 © AP/Wide World Photos; p. 85 digital image © 1996 Corbis, original image courtesy of NASA/Corbis.

Designer: Les Kanturek; Editor: John Kemmerer